Turning Your Trash Into Treasure

A Guide to Selling Online

Priscilla Benfield

This book is dedicated to my family whose never-ending support means everything to me.

Table of Contents

Forward

Do you want to downsize or maybe you just need some extra cash? Selling your unwanted items online is a great way to get rid of unwanted "stuff" and earn some money.

There are many how-to guides promising to show you how to earn money selling online so why read mine?

After some major financial setbacks in my life I was looking for a way to earn some extra cash from the comfort of my own home. I explored every option and found that selling unwanted items online was something that I not only enjoyed doing but was good at.

There are many things that people will pay money for and this guide will divulge some of those surprising items. Who knows what you have hiding in the back of a closet or lost in your attic? No matter how organized we are, no matter how we might like to think we have clutter under control there is money to be found in everyone's home.

After many years of selling online on sites like eBay and Etsy I have learned a lot about selling online. This guide is a how-to for those of you who have stuff and want to make some money from it.

Let's get started!

Introduction

Maybe your house doesn't look like you should be on "Hoarders" but let's face it- living the day-to-day life we all do can get crazy. Children grow up in the blink of an eye and they outgrow stuff. Sometimes we are able to keep up on getting rid of things and sometimes we tuck it away thinking we might need it. The same goes for people who don't have children. "Stuff" just accumulates.

If you have a collection that started off small, I'll bet that at some point it has gotten out of control. Selling off part of a collection is always a good way to earn some extra money.

Selling online takes organization, sometimes long hours and dedication but it can be a source of extra income that most people are looking for.

The most surprising thing I have found as I have been selling online is just what sells. There is truth to the old saying "One man's trash is another man's treasure". Keep that in mind as you look in your basement or storage area for things to sell online.

There are many parts to selling online and I will explore, explain and give tips for just how to do it in this book.

Why sell online

I've done yard sales and honestly I will never do one again. You wake up early in the morning, drag your belongings outside and then wait. Even if you have done your prep work by advertising and preparing your items for sale, selling items in a yard sale is hit or miss. You cannot control the weather and even if it is a perfect weather day, maybe people just aren't buying that day. At the end of the day you have to drag all that stuff back into your house and you spent the entire day hanging around outside hoping to make a few bucks. Seldom is it worth it.

Flea markets are the same except you have to pay a fee to rent the space to showcase your stuff for sale. Even if you have a vehicle large enough to tote all your stuff to the venue, it still is a pain to do it. Then you have to worry about how you will set it up and are the buyers coming out on that particular day.

If you are just interested in spending your day chit-chatting with your neighbors, throw a barbecue. Flea markets and yard/tag sales are a waste of valuable time in my opinion.

In my world time is money. I like to use my time wisely and to my best advantage. It makes no sense to me to spend several hours outside trying to sell my used goods to my neighbors when I can list the same items online reaching many more people thus increasing the chance that I will make a sale.

Many times items I list for sale are purchased by people in areas of the country where my item might be harder to find. This is just one of the things to consider about selling items online.

A few years back my mother had a bunch of VHS movies that she didn't want. She tried selling them in a yard sale here in New Jersey but no one looked twice at them. She gave them to my sister who lives in Tennessee. She easily sold them in a yard sale. This is an example of how different items are more valuable in different areas of the country.

There are some items that I just wouldn't even bother trying to sell locally but listing them online advertises them to a much larger audience thereby increasing the chance of making a sale.

I currently only sell to the lower 48 United States but in the future I plan on widening my range. I just do not have the time right now to deal with customs forms and the extra work that international selling entails.

Working from home perks

Selling online gives you the advantage of working for yourself from the comfort of your own home in your own time. The Internet is open 24/7 so if you are a night owl or an early bird it doesn't matter. Selling online is perfect as a second job because you do it when it is convenient for you!

If you have the space for a home office great, but honestly you do not even need one. I sell handmade items in an Etsy store and also sell Vintage and used items on eBay all from my "office" which doubles as my living room!

After I first lost my job many years ago and had trouble finding something else I explored many opportunities for working from home. So many of them were scams or made outrageous promises. I did web content writing and I also did customer service work for a Halloween costume company. Selling items online is the only "job" I found where I am 100% in charge of my success or failure.

I have not been able to replace a steady paycheck with selling unwanted items online but I have been able to successfully supplement my family's income. It is possible to make a living selling online but teaching you how to do that is not the goal of this book. The goal is to make some cash selling unwanted items that you already have around your house.

How do you sell online?

Organization is the key. I do not have a large home but I do make the best possible use out of the space that I do have.

Maybe you think that you don't have time to sell online. If you have items that you don't want and you want to do more than donate them, selling them online is the best option. You can get organized and you can sell them online without a lot of effort.

Maybe your goal is to just make some extra cash for a much-needed vacation and you have a few items you want to sell.

You might have a larger inventory of stuff; maybe your late aunt left you with boxes of vintage items that you don't want or need.

Whatever your story is this guide can help you to get started selling online.

I have held down a full-time job and still have been able to make time to successfully sell online. You do need to be somewhat organized but once all the hard work is done, selling online can be as simple as checking your e-mail.

We live in the Internet age. I know that many people are afraid of the Internet. Many people think they are not computer literate enough to sell online. Believe me you are literate enough to do this. It isn't hard to learn how to sell online.

The Internet makes it easy to promote your items for sale thereby increasing the odds of selling them.

You will need a computer and a bank account for starters. If you have a home printer (which most of us do) you can print your own postage from home and save time.

What you earn depends upon many factors. I do not promise that you will become rich but you will be able to earn some extra cash for stuff that you no longer want. Everyone needs extra cash, don't they?

What about overhead?

The cost of selling online varies. My costs are very low. It does take some know-how to keep your selling costs at the absolute minimum. More information on this will come later on in the book.

The majority of the items I sell online did not cost me anything. The stuff I have sold that was purchased by me is things that I no longer want, need or have any use for. My mindset with many items is that whatever I can get for them outweighs any usefulness for having them around. I don't sell stuff that I don't need. I sell stuff I don't want.

If you are emotionally attached to an item it will be much more difficult to sell it. Emotional attachment often causes a person to overvalue an item. In my journey I have learned that what you believe an item is worth is often wrong. Worth of an item depends upon many factors.

We will explore this in detail later on but now we will focus on shipping costs.

In some of my listings I state my shipping policies. On eBay there are sellers who offer free shipping. Many of them are large companies who ship from China or Hong Kong. They sell large amounts of product and they can afford to not charge for shipping. You will also wait 10 days or more for your item. I remind prospective buyers that I am just a girl from Jersey trying to supplement my family's income. I ship fast and I only charge what it costs to ship an item.

As my feedback shows, my customers appreciate receiving their items fast.

I ship within 1 business day because when I buy something online I want it now! I don't make money from shipping because I don't believe it is right. I use recycled packaging whenever I can and that is one way that I keep my costs low.

Although my main goal is to get rid of stuff, I also want to make a profit.

Maybe you are unable to ship out next day. That's okay. I have also seen some sellers who only ship on Saturdays. Depending on how you list an item, it is relatively easy to plan out when you are available to ship.

If you are only going to sell auction-style on eBay, determining when you want to ship items is easy. Just list your items so that the listing end falls within the time frame you need to get paid and then ship. The only thing that can go wrong here is when a buyer doesn't pay right away. In a perfect eBay world, the buyer pays within a few hours and it works out for you.

When you are trying to juggle your life and you are just learning how to sell online, trips to the post office might not be convenient. If you are opting to not ship from home, you will have to figure out what will work with your schedule. Depending upon your work hours and ability to get to the post office, it can be challenging to figure out how you are going to manage.

During the holiday season I was forced to go to the post office to ship out some items. My printer wasn't working and I had items to ship. On my wish list is a new printer because I do not want to have to do that again!

Juggling boxes and standing in long lines waiting for people who were sending out last-minute gifts is not how I want to spend my free time.

If you aren't selling many items, going to the post office now and again isn't horrible. When you are selling several items a week, shipping from home is smarter.

What should I sell?

A better question to ask is what do you have? If you are focused on just making money then this guide might not be for you. You can make money selling unwanted items online but you will not get rich from it unless of course your family has an attic full of priceless heirlooms. Most of us don't but that doesn't mean you don't have items worth money.

Start by taking mental inventory of what you have that you don't want. You can even go one step further and get a pad and a pen and start writing it all down.

Go from room to room and look around. It might surprise you what you have right under your nose that you are willing to part with. The mistake you can make is thinking that something isn't worth selling. Many times you are wrong in your thinking. There really is a market for just about anything. It might not be worth a lot of money, but it is worth something.

After you have several items written down, the next step is to investigate what these items are actually worth.

Go to eBay.com with your list and one by one, start your research. You do not need to have an eBay account to do this. Signing up on eBay (or other sites) will come later.

In the search bar type in what the item is. You will see how many similar items are currently listed for sale. Choose one of the listings and notice what the starting bid is, if there are any bids on it and how the seller is showing it. Read the description of the item and take a good look at the pictures the seller is using.

I sometimes will bookmark an item if I feel that I can refer to it when selling my own item that is similar. You can also take notes in a notebook but bookmarking it gives you all the info you need and it saves time later.

There are many factors to consider when selling an item on eBay. You will increase your chances of selling if you portray the item honestly. How do you portray an item honestly?

1- Take a good quality picture of the item (use natural light whenever possible!)
2- Describe the item! This means detail! Measure it, weigh it, give history of the item- you can never say enough.
3- Know the true value of the item. This means research what the item has sold for recently and just how many of them are available.

Selling on eBay can be intimidating. There are so many categories and sometimes you might wonder how to get your item to stand out.

You might think that your listing is going to get lost in the huge amount of "stuff" for sale on eBay. It can. What helps is using the right words to list the item and knowing how and when to promote it.

eBay will send you messages giving you suggestions on how to sell your item. Often they will suggest that your item could be presented better with an updated photo. Other times the suggestion has to do with the price. Selling auction-style is tricky. If you start an item at too low of a bid and there is little interest you might be giving it away to one lucky buyer. If you start too high you run the risk of turning off potential buyers.

For moments like these when you are unsure of how to start an auction, look around and see what others are doing.

Ebay allows you to sell at either a fixed price or auction. Fixed price also has the option of adding a "best offer" which can be helpful if you really want a certain amount of money and you want to increase the chances of it selling faster.

Auctions last for 3, 5 or 7 days. If the item gets a bid you have to wait until the auction time is over to finalize the sale. This can be good because often other buyers get in on the bidding.

Selling as a fixed price is good in two ways. If you don't feel like being tied in to waiting for an auction to end and you want to ensure you get a certain amount of money, fixed price listings are for you. Adding the option of a best offer accepted makes it more flexible. The other way a fixed price listing is good is because you can list it until it is sold.

Some items take longer to sell. Many times eBay will tell you it is because of your price. Sometimes it is. I have learned that many times it is simply because the right buyer hasn't found it yet.

I use the three strikes you're out rule. I list (either as an auction or fixed price) and allow it to go three cycles. If the item doesn't sell I reevaluate it. Sometimes I will switch it and list it as an auction if I had no luck as a fixed listing. There are other times where I simply put the item away and return to it a few weeks later.

Selling online can sometimes be hit or miss. I have learned to be patient with listings that seem to sit. Things will sell when the right buyer comes along.

Preparing to list

Before you get into the actual process of listing items for sale online you need to think about what you are selling and what you hope to gain. The biggest thing I have learned is to let go of my expectations of what an item is worth until I do the research. Being emotionally attached to an item can cause you to sabotage your selling efforts. Let go of the personal history attached to an item and you will do much better!

After years of selling online my mindset has changed. When I list an item for sale my main goal is to rid myself of the item. If it turns out to be a "hot" item – great, if I am able to earn something off of it I am happy. Sometimes you need to remind yourself that you didn't want the item anymore so anything earned is a step forward.

Where to sell

I sell online on Craigslist, Etsy and eBay. I will break down these three sites and explain what I feel each site is best for.

Craigslist

Craigslist is good for items that I sell locally. Items like large furniture or items that would be costly to ship I prefer to list on Craigslist. I never ever post my phone number and instead have prospective buyers contact me through email.

This site is free to list items on and very easy to use. You will need an e-mail address to post a listing. Items can get "lost" on Craigslist but they now have an option where you can push the listing to the top of the page if it remains for sale too long.

I use Craigslist only when I absolutely have to because like yard sales, selling on Craigslist can be a waste of time. Arranging a time and place to meet prospective buyers can be a nuisance but if you absolutely must sell something (like a mini-fridge) that would be cumbersome to ship, Craigslist is the best option.

When I list something for sale on Craigslist I know that prospective buyers are going to bargain on the price much like someone would do at a yard sale. That's fine with me. I expect this and that is why my asking price is slightly higher than what I expect to get.

If you are firm on what you want for an item the best thing to do is put your asking price slightly higher knowing that you will only accept a certain amount.

Etsy

Etsy is a site where many artists sell their art but it is also a great place for selling craft supplies or Vintage items. The downside of Etsy is that it costs .20 for each listing (for 3 months). It doesn't have as wide of an audience as eBay but if your focus is just on homemade items it is the place to sell.

When you sign up on Etsy you automatically have a store. There is no charge to open a store but there is a charge for listing items. Etsy is a good option for selling online but for getting items sold now, eBay is the best choice.

In order to sell successfully on Etsy you will need to build up an audience and if you have a strong social media following, go for it. If not, go the easier way and start selling on eBay.

Listings on Etsy are fixed price which can take longer to sell.

eBay

Listing auction style is free on eBay but auctions aren't the only way to sell on eBay. You can sell at a fixed price but it does cost .30 for each listing.

Both eBay and Etsy charge a fee when the item sells- the cost is a percentage of the selling price. (Check out FAQ's for sellers on both sites)

EBay often runs specials where you can list a certain amount of items for free or sometimes upgrades like extra photos are free. Ebay will send you e-mails notifying you of these promotions and I always try and take advantage of them.

I like selling auction style for many of my items. It is not unusual for a 7-day auction listing to be re-listed before it sells but for most of my listings they do sell within a 3 week period. When they don't sell in this time period I reevaluate the listing.

Ebay does charge fees to sell. Seller fees are due once a month. To avoid having a huge bill, pay your fees as you go. Once an item sells, ship it and then pay the seller fee to eBay. It is a small percentage of what the item sells for. Honestly it hurts less to pay your fees this way especially in the beginning when you have just starting selling.

When I first started selling on eBay I thought that the fees were excessive. As time went on and I learned more about eBay I started to change my mind. As a seller, eBay offers a lot of support. From suggestions on how to sell an item to backing me up when a buyer has a dispute, the fees that I pay are a small price.

Choosing auction style or fixed price

I use fixed price when I am sure of how much an item is worth and when I am pretty set in what I want to get for it.

It does often take longer to sell at a fixed price but this is something you need to consider when you sell online. Are you looking for cash right now or can you wait?

Ebay will almost always suggest that you start an auction at .99. I disagree with this. For some items, .99 is all you are going to get and that is sometimes unacceptable. If there are many similar items listed and yours is listed with a starting bid of .99 you might see it rise to a price more favorable to you but that is not always the way it goes. I start items at .99 when I honestly just want to sell them and do not care if the bid goes up.

You can start an auction at .99 but have a reserve price set. This is a way to ensure that you are not giving the item away. Some buyers will not bother with an auction with a reserve price. In my opinion you should be sure that your item is worthy of the reserve price and only then should you use it.

Auctions on eBay can favor the buyer or the seller. There are guides out there that might promise you different but the truth is that auctions can be a gamble.

So why sell on eBay?

There are many sites online that appear to be an alternative to selling on eBay. The truth is that eBay gives your items the best exposure without a lot of work on your part. It is more trusted and it does have a good support system for sellers as well as for buyers.

My tips for selling can be used on any site where you want to sell things. The reason I sell mostly on eBay is because of the exposure that I get there.

To sell on eBay you need an e-mail account and a PayPal account. I have used PayPal for years and you might have read complaints or known people who don't like it. Personally I have had no issues with PayPal. These days so many of us shop online and with so many sites using PayPal, chances are good that you probably have an account.

Shipping

Part of selling an item online is getting it to your buyer. Maybe this part of selling online scares people but it shouldn't be the reason why you don't try selling online.

Shipping is just a matter of packing the item up and choosing a shipping method. I ship via the USPS because it is what I know and I am satisfied with it.

I recycle shipping supplies whenever possible. I also take advantage of free shipping supplies. I buy shipping supplies only when I have to and when I have to I shop smart. What are you going to need to get your items to your buyers? A lot depends upon what you are going to sell.

The first thing you need to consider is will you physically be going to your local post office or will you ship from home?

Early on I learned that shipping from home was much more cost effective. I got a USPS approved postal scale and print my postage at home. Printing your own postage saves money versus going to the post office and paying for it there. Also it saves time. (my time is money after all!)

Another perk to printing your own postage is when you ship via the USPS and use Priority shipping you can request a pick-up. The post office will come to your home and pick up your packages. This is especially great when the weather is nasty!

My tip for making shipping easier is to plan ahead. I put aside boxes that I receive from purchases online and I save things like bubble wrap and other packing materials. I buy packing tape in bulk which costs less than buying it a roll at a time. I've also purchased brown heavy-duty wrapping from the dollar store to have for wrapping custom-made boxes.

I order free shipping boxes from the USPS and try to always have a variety of sizes on hand. Be careful when choosing free boxes from the USPS. Avoid the flat rate boxes. In my opinion medium and large flat rate boxes are not a good value. The cost of shipping with the postal service has steadily gone up. A better choice is to get the standard Priority rate boxes and use them. If by chance it is cheaper to use standard shipping I still use the priority mail box but I wrap it in brown craft paper. The post office will not allow you to use a USPS Priority mail box to ship anything but Priority mail.

Go to USPS.com and sign up for a free account. You can order free shipping boxes from their site which your mailman will deliver to your door!

I am fortunate that I have a basement where I can store my shipping supplies. If your space is limited consider breaking down boxes and storing them under a bed or in a closet. Aside from my basement I do not have a home office but I manage to keep supplies on hand to run my business pretty effectively.

In addition to boxes to ship the item in you also will need packing materials. Some people use newspaper but I am always concerned about newsprint rubbing off and causing damage.

Tissue paper, wrapping paper and plastic grocery bags make good packing material. If you have a shredder you can shred last Christmas' wrapping paper for packing material. Store it in a plastic garbage bag so it is ready to use.

If a lot of your items are fragile, invest in a large roll of bubble wrap which you can purchase from an office supply store. You need to make sure that your item gets to your buyer in one piece. Overwrapping is never a bad thing!

The only expense I do recommend is buying a postage scale. This way you can purchase and print shipping from the comfort of your own home. A good quality scale can be purchased at Walmart for around $25. You will also need packing tape and depending upon what you are selling, packing materials.

When you list items for sale you will also need to know how much the item weighs (packed and ready to ship weight) so you can add that to the price of the item. More on this later but this is why a postage scale is necessary.

What to sell and how to get ready

So you have identified a few items you want to sell and you have researched their worth according to eBay. What's next?

Your picture of the item and your description of it are essential to selling the item. The first thing you need to do is to prepare the item for this process.

Most of the items I sell are found discarded in basements and attics. Years of neglect can leave items dusty, smelly and sometimes in conditions that might not be worthy of being sold. The first thing you need to do is clean the item up!

Clothing should be washed to get out any musty smell. Sometimes some minor mending might be needed after laundering.

When cleaning out my parents' attic I found a child's dress from the mid-60s. I remember this dress from pictures and decided I could clean it up and sell it in my Etsy store. I brought it home and soaked it in the washing machine and then allowed it to air-dry. The washing process made the hem come down but I painstakingly re-hemmed the dress. It was only after hemming that I noticed some small (but now very noticeable) holes in the fabric from moths. I was devastated. I spent too much time preparing this item only to see that selling it in this condition was a waste of my time.

I haven't yet thrown the item out; instead it sits in a box because I still believe there might be another life for it yet.

The point is that you have to make educated decisions about what you are going to spend time on. Maybe there was a little bit too much sentiment involved with the velvet dress and I didn't examine it carefully.

Why waste time on an old vintage child's dress? If I had been able to clean it up, it definitely would have sold. There is a market out there for vintage clothing.

On that same find I discovered a paper bag with infants' shoes. They were used and pretty beat up. I wiped them down and sold them for $6 a pair.

Anything you find around your house that you are going to sell online needs to be cleaned up before you sell it. You are going to be taking pictures of it and a clean item is going to be more attractive than something that looks dirty and neglected. It's just common sense.

Recently I took advantage of a town-wide yard sale just because I enjoy a good find. As I looked around I was observing what people try to sell and how they go about it. When you are selling something used the way to make it sell is to present it well. At one sale it seemed that the seller did no preparation for their sale. All they did was to empty out their garage. The items were scattered on the ground and many of the items were covered in dirt and dust.

It was not easy for anything to catch my eye. It all looked like garbage. If you are not going to bother with preparing an item to sell than you are sabotaging the chances of selling it.

If the item is vintage, gentle cleaning is best. If the item is used but newer, your focus should be on shining it up to make it look like new.

Especially with vintage items, think gentle when cleaning. Sometimes all you need is to wipe something with a damp cloth. Use cleaners like a spray bottle with white vinegar and water on hard surfaces. Most jewelry will clean up using mild detergent, a toothbrush and cloth to dry it.

Hand wash delicate fabrics and let air dry.

Even newer items can collect dust so clean them up before you take the next step in the selling process.

When you sell online your description of what you are selling needs to be spot-on. Getting a good picture of the item is the next step.

After trial-and-error, I have learned that the best pictures are taken in natural light. I am not a photographer, nor do I possess a natural ability to take a good picture so taking a good photo is an on-going challenge for me.

When I first started I used a camera borrowed from my daughter. Today I use my iPhone4. I do manage to capture my items pretty well.

It is difficult at times to get the perfect shot. I plan out when I am going to take pictures. I keep a bin where I place items that have been cleaned and readied for sale. I am a morning person so I head outside very early in the morning and set up on my porch.

Once colder weather sets in I am forced to take photos inside. It still takes me longer to get a good picture inside but I am always learning.

Make sure to not have shadows or sun glare which will ruin the picture. Use a background that will compliment the item. You want the item to pop. I have used tablecloths, china, and even pillowcases to serve as backdrops.

I sell handmade wreaths in my Etsy store and many of them have beautiful shiny ornaments on them. When I first started selling them I was so pleased when I captured their beauty and then on second glance noticed my reflection in one of the shiny ornaments in the photo.

I have seen many people make the same mistake. Just as a writer needs to proofread, a photographer needs to also. At first glance the wreath looked good until I looked closer and saw myself in it!

I re-shot the pictures using a different angle and made a mental note to be mindful of capturing myself in future pictures.

Depending upon what you are selling, you should have at the very least 3 good photos of the item. Sometimes just one photo is enough but it depends upon what the item is. For the holiday wreaths I sell I usually post two- one of the whole wreath and a second one of the detail close-up.

Many of the items I sell are vintage. People who love vintage items do not expect to get a brand-new item. Often vintage items have signs of wear. Ever hear the saying "a picture says 1,000 words"? This is so true when selling online.

I try and include the best possible shots of the item from different angles. Take a book for example. I would take a picture of the cover, the back, from the side where you could see the pages and if there was any kinds of damage on the inside cover I would take pictures of that.

You have to cover yourself for the buyer who doesn't pay attention and also for the buyer who is interested in what you have but just needs a push to be sold.

Don't be afraid that this sounds like a time-consuming process. It does get easier with practice.

I recommend starting off slowly. Do your photos of one or two items and then follow through with the listing process. Once you get more experienced you can do more.

Organization helps. I use a series of plastic bins to streamline the listing/selling process.

I have a bin of stuff that needs pictures, a bin of stuff to be prepared for photos and then once an item is listed it goes in a separate bin while it waits to be sold.

It can be tough to remember where you left off in the listing process so having a system helps.

Don't rush the process of taking photos. If you are photo-challenged like I am you will need to resist the urge to settle for a less than perfect shot. Getting a good picture helps greatly in selling the item.

Natural light does capture items best but again, freezing temperatures make it impossible to take a picture outside.

There is somewhere in your home where you can set up a photo studio to take a good picture. It might take a bit of trial and error but you will find it.

In the beginning it is time-consuming to sell online. You are learning the ropes so remember this and be patient.

Your hard work will pay off.

After your pictures have been taken to your satisfaction you need to upload them to your computer and save them. When I save my photos I usually give the item and name and then number them in the order I will use them. For example I was listing a pearl necklace. I labeled the best picture "pearlmain" and each picture after that I labeled "pearl1", "pearl2", etc.

Although eBay gives you up to 12 photos for free for a basic listing, I rarely need more than 5 per item. I do like to use the best photo as the main photo.

See the help section on eBay for specifics on size photos allowed.

Pictures don't tell the whole story

A good picture will help sell the item but the description is another part of the process. Once I have taken the pictures I set myself up with the tools I need to start listing.

Often I will take notes of what similar items are selling for and now that it is time to list them, my notes will be a valuable help. I also check my bookmarks for anything I might have noticed while researching the going price for an item.

I gather my listing tools and get started. I have a notebook that I use for everything from notes on an item to reminders of similar listings, a tape measure, my scale and a magnifying glass.

Why a magnifying glass? Much of the items I sell were not mine. Many times I am not sure of their history and often I cannot tell just by looking if a piece of jewelry is costume or fine. Magnifying glasses have saved me many times from selling something as "junk" when it was actually 18k gold. It is also helpful for finding a copyright in an old book or the year on the back of a Barbie doll.

Details are important and can make or break a sale. Listing an item is when you give them all the info you have and hope it is what they are looking for.

People like precise measurements so use a tape measure and include the exact size of an item in your description.

If you don't measure it, chances are someone is going to ask for the measurements. It is a time-saver to take care of all the details right away.

Describing your item is important but you also need to sell it through your words. You need to make the item sound irresistible.

There is a fine line here. eBay holds their sellers to standards. The item your buyer receives must be as described. If it is not the buyer is entitled to a refund even if you do not offer any. Always do your best to describe the item as it is.

I've worked really hard to get to the top seller level on eBay. I pay attention to every detail when I am writing my listings and I do my best to describe the item accurately. I have learned how to protect myself against unscrupulous buyers. There are people out there who will try and leave negative feedback or demand a refund unjustly.

This is why I am so adamant about detail. Along with precise measurements and offering all the information I know about an item, I also make sure that if I do not know something about the item, I state it in the listing.

Describing the item so there are no surprises when the buyer receives it is the universal rule to selling online. It doesn't matter what site you are selling your stuff on. Every buyer expects to receive what you describe the item to be. There are exceptions of course.

One year I sold a wreath and the feedback from the buyer still bothers me. The buyer complained that it was the "ugliest" wreath and had she "known" that she would never have bought it. At first my artist's feelings were hurt but then I regained my senses. I had included several pictures of the wreath in my listing and the wreath was exactly as pictured. Did the buyer purchase it without even looking at the pictures? Why would you purchase something without looking at it?

When I thought about it I had to laugh. Then I decided that anyone who would read this feedback would think the same thing as me. I decided not to worry about her negative feedback.

Even if your goal is to just sell off a few items from a prized collection you still need to be concerned about feedback. You want your buyer to be happy. A happy buyer might buy from you again. A buyer who is pleased with his purchase and leaves positive feedback is free promotion for you.

I have learned that staying organized and paying attention to detail makes selling online easier. Proofread what you have written and look at your photos as if you have never seen the item before.

Try and imagine that you are the buyer. Ask yourself "am I answering all possible questions that a buyer might have"?

Another way to sell an item is to suggest how it could be used. There are many artsy people who re-purpose items that many of us think of as junk. Odd pieces from an old board game, mis-matched silverware, the list of treasures is endless. There is value for just about anything to the right person.

When you sell online you have a greater chance of finding the right buyer for these "odd" items.

What is my stuff really worth?

What you can get for your item and what you want to get for your item are often two different amounts. The first rule is to remove any emotional attachments that you have to the item. This helps greatly in accepting that your item is not actually worth what you thought.

My mom had a huge collection of Elvis Presley memorabilia. When my parents recently packed up their belongings to move after 50+ years in their home she realized she needed to downsize some of her collections. She believed that she had items that were worth a good amount of money. Much to her surprise after doing research I had to tell her she was wrong.

Many collectible items are mass produced which makes them not as valuable as one would assume. The other factor in making her collectibles not as valuable is the fact that they are widely available.

The bottom line is that if you are serious about down-sizing your collection you might need to accept the idea that you are not going to get as much money for it as you hoped. If you are so emotionally attached that you cannot accept that, keep the item and let go of something else instead.

The condition of your item also is a factor in determining its worth. Just because the item has damage does not mean that it isn't worth something.

Many vintage items are worth a lot more when they are still in the original packaging. Just because it was removed and used doesn't mean that it has no worth. Surprisingly if someone really wants it, many times they don't care about the original packaging.

I have had brand-new items take forever to sell but seen beat-up old Monopoly pieces sell quickly. You never know what someone is looking for. Never assume that there is no worth in something. The monetary value might not be what you are expecting but it will still be worth something.

Using eBay to research recent sales of a similar item is helpful in knowing what your odds are of selling. Check completed listings and also check current listings. It might sound like a lot of work but it isn't. Once you start to get familiar with the site you will learn a lot about online selling.

The many ways you can sabotage your selling efforts

The biggest mistake is over or under valuing the item. Getting rid of the item is a goal but you also want to earn money from doing so.

You cannot blindly sell an item without risking giving it away. You have to research it.

The other way to sabotage your selling efforts is through your listing of the item. Details are important and can make the difference between an item that sells and an item that sits.

Honesty in selling is not only important for your reputation as a seller but in your success in getting rid of your unwanted items. When you present an item clearly and honestly it increases the chances of it getting sold.

There are other factors in selling online that you have absolutely no control over. Once you accept this fact selling online will become easier.

There are no guarantees that what you have someone wants. But, and this might sound overly optimistic (but it is not) if it is not out there it won't sell either!

You never know what someone is looking for at any given time. You can try and follow the seasonal rules when selling but again, there are exceptions.

You might think that someone is not going to purchase Christmas decorations in July but if it is priced right someone might.

I sold old National Geographic magazines when I first started selling online. Some sold very quickly and others I put away because they seemed un-sellable. Obviously the ones that sold were issues that someone was looking for. There are a lot of National Geographic magazines for sale on the Internet but if you are looking for a specific issue you might have a harder time finding it. I had the ones that someone wanted so I made money selling them.

Having an item that someone wants is only part of the equation. Selling it at a price that someone is willing to pay is the other part.

How do you price it right so that you sell it at a profit? Research and luck. Plain and simple.

Getting down to selling

You have prepared your item for sale. The pictures have been taken; research on what it is worth is done. What do you do next?

If it is a large item (think over 50 lbs or very bulky) selling it locally using Craigslist is your best option. You could sell it on eBay listing it as a local pick-up only but you will get greater exposure using Craigslist.

Craigslist is very user friendly. You will need an e-mail address to sell something on the site.

Listing on Craigslist is similar to listing anywhere else online in that you will need to sell your item through your pictures of it and your written description of the item.

Before you do place your ad, you should look around on Craigslist to see what others are asking for a similar item. Craigslist does suggest you post a picture with what you are selling but I have seen people try and sell without a picture. If I am buying something online I want to see a picture and not just read a description.

Their categories are simpler than a larger site like eBay. It is free to list so if you have an item like Grandma's china set you can easily list it in two categories like "Antiques" and "Household" in order to get more exposure.

Whatever you do, remember good pictures & good description + a fair price= a better chance of selling.

Your prospective buyer will be meeting you in person to finalize the sale but state in your ad that you accept cash only. Do not accept checks- even money orders can be forged or faked.

When selling on Craigslist I always consider when is the best time to post so that it will get the highest exposure.

I've gotten most of my sales on the weekends. Listing early on a Saturday morning or a Friday night always seemed to work best for me.

If you will be listing an item on any other site, you will need a PayPal account in order to get paid. You need a bank account or major credit card to get a PayPal account. It is simple to do and secure.

Go to PayPal.com and set up a personal account. It is free to do and PayPal only charges a fee when you get paid for selling an item. The fees are small. PayPal charges 2.9% per transaction. They send you an e-mail when you receive a payment and you can always log into your account to see your balance and fees charged. You can also use PayPal to ship an item but I ship directly through eBay which I find easier.

If the item is smaller signing up for an account on eBay is your best option. Registering on eBay is also easy.

Listing an item for sale on eBay

eBay is very user-friendly even for those who feel computer challenged.

Setting up your PayPal account should be done before you register on eBay. Once you have set up your PayPal account, next is registering on eBay.

You can come up with a cutesy user name or just use whatever name that you might have an existing online presence with. This will help later on when you are promoting your items for sale.

eBay also charges fees for selling. The first 50 items you list auction-style in a month are free to list. You do pay a fee when they sell. The final value fee is about 10% of the final selling price plus the shipping cost that the buyer pays. See eBay for more details. There is a difference in costs for selling an item at a fixed price versus auction style. As I stated before, this is not a guide exclusive to selling on eBay.

After you have registered for accounts with PayPal and eBay, it is time to list your item for sale.

What category do I use?

The first thing you will need to do after logging in to your account is to choose what category you will be selling in. You should already know what category to use from doing your research on similar items for sale.

Ebay can seem overwhelming especially when you are trying to figure out what category to list your item in. You can choose more than one category but there is a fee to list in more than one category. I prefer to use a category that others selling similar items were successful in. If after going through a few weeks of not selling an item you can always re-list it and change the category.

The title

Your picture helps to sell your item but a good title is what will grab the buyer's attention. You get up to 80 characters to use in your title. Here is where your research helps. Seeing how others sold a similar item can help you in listing.

I sell many vintage items online. If you are selling something and it is already listed in a category of vintage items, you do not need to repeat "vintage" in your title. A buyer of vintage items is already looking in the category. Save the space for a description of what the item is.

Think about what is special/unique/different about the item. I have sold many vintage Sarah Coventry jewelry pieces. It is costume jewelry but it was very well-made. Collectors of these pieces know what they are looking for. Using the name of the piece in the title as well as pointing out what makes it special helped me to attract the right buyer.

Give a lot of thought to your title. If your item isn't selling, eBay will make the suggestion that you revise your title.

Condition description

You must identify the exact condition of an item. In this space I normally put "read description and see photos for detail". This protects me against a buyer who might try to dispute a sale.

Photos

You are allowed up to 12 photos for an item. Anything more will cost money but rarely will you need more than 12.

On average I use 4 photos for a listing. If your photo is not a good quality photo, eBay will reject it. For more on photo sizes allowed, see the help section.

Item specifics

In many categories there will be drop-down choices for item specifics. This is very helpful for selling because it makes your item easier to find.

If you do not know for sure you can choose "unknown" or something similar. At least you will not be giving out false information.

I always repeat item specifics in the body of the listing.

Details

You cannot say enough about the item for sale. Do not rely upon the pictures to tell the whole story. A good picture is necessary but what you say about the item is also essential.

When I sell a necklace (for example) I state what it is made of. Is it real gold or just gold-plated? How long is it? Is there a gemstone and if so, how large is it? Is it in working condition? If the clasp is broken, it is not un-sellable!

In my listing after I have described the item I also request that buyers ask questions before they bid or purchase the item. This is just my way of warning people that you get what you pay for and if you are unsure that this item is for you, you need to ask questions before you buy.

I also explain my shipping policy. Although later on in the listing there is a drop-down choice of how fast you will ship the item and the shipping process you use, I spell it all out for the buyer.

I state that I only charge actual cost of shipping and I do not make money from shipping costs. Sometimes I even explain that I recycle shipping materials to so I do not have to pass on the cost to the buyer but this isn't necessary.

Choosing a format and price

This is where you choose to either sell at auction or a fixed price. From doing your research you already should know what to do. Set your starting auction price or fixed price.

Select how you will be paid

This is easy. I always (only) choose PayPal to process my payments.

Shipping

You need to know approximately how much it is going to cost to ship the item when you list it for sale. This is where a novice seller can run into trouble. Selling a necklace and shipping it will cost less money than shipping a mug. Shipping charges vary according to where it is going and how much it weighs.

Pre-package your item for accuracy and to save time.

You want to make sure that the item is going to arrive in one piece and how you pack it makes a difference.

Look at your item and place get it ready to be shipped. You do not need to seal the box but act as if you are ready to ship it. Weigh it and put the approximate weight in. eBay automatically will give you a range of the cost according to the service and method you choose.

Priority mail from the USPS is what I most often use. The USPS has flat rate shipping charges and special boxes but flat rate box rates are not available for all destinations.

Because of this (and the high cost of using medium and large flat rate boxes) I avoid using it. You can only use First Class mail for packages that are less than one pound.

I have learned (through trial and error) the approximate cost of shipping certain items that I sell. I live on the East coast and to send something across the country can be expensive. When the item sells I can see exactly how much the cost is because I now know where it needs to go to.

You do not want any profit you make from the sale of your item go towards sending the item to the buyer. This is why you need to weigh the package and estimate what it will cost to send it.

The invoice will be adjusted to reflect the exact cost of postage but you need to put the weight of the package in at the time you list the item. Get the weight wrong and it can really mess you up!

Estimating the weight of a package is something that you do get better at with experience. Hopefully it doesn't cost you to lose profits while you learn.

You also have the option of international shipping but I only ship to the lower 48 United States. When you are first starting out selling online, keep it simple.

Buyer requirements

eBay's listing tools make it easy to be specific about who you will sell to. I always opt to only sell to buyers who have a PayPal account. I also opt out of selling to buyers outside of the United States. I further protect myself by only selling to buyers who do not have policy violations.

Returns

eBay now requires sellers to state up front what their policy is regarding returns. I do accept returns on many of the items I sell but I do state that the buyer is responsible for the cost of return shipping.

To make sure that your sale will be final make sure to describe the item fully and completely.

On the next page you will review the listing and make any changes. It will show you any fees for the listing such as upgrades like bold print and additional photos. Then you can choose list your item.

You can go back and revise the listing if you need to. The only time you cannot make changes is when the listing is nearing the end.

The listing is live, now what?

Promoting your items for sale

Social media makes it easy to promote your items for sale and helps to get views. The more views your item gets the better the chances of finding a buyer for it. eBay is huge and it is easy for your item to get lost.

I use Twitter, Facebook, Pinterest and my personal blogs to promote what I am selling online. Once your item is listed you can share it directly from your listing by either sending it to a friend via e-mail, tweeting it, sharing it on your Facebook page or pinning it on Pinterest.

It is easy to link any of your accounts to your eBay seller account to promote your item.

Many sellers even have a Facebook page to promote their items. If you plan on making this a permanent hobby/second job, creating a Facebook page is a great way to promote your efforts.

While I wait for items to sell I do promote them daily. I use social media to gain views and I also follow other sellers who sell similar items.

Networking on the Internet is easy and you can learn a lot from more experienced sellers. Most of us already use social media so it is not a foreign thing to do.

I always have had a passion for Vintage items and I have connected online with people who share that passion. I promote their items and they return the favor.

You can find a fan site for just about anything these days. Connecting online with others who appreciate or collect stuff you are looking to sell can help you sell faster.

Using social media isn't necessary to sell your unwanted items online but it does help. Signing up for these accounts is easy to do and it is free.

The item sells – what to do next?

When your item sells you will receive an e-mail notifying you if you are using a site like eBay or Etsy. eBay and other sites (except Craigslist) automatically sends an invoice to the buyer but I always send one also.

At this time you know where you need to send the item and you will have a clearer picture of what the shipping charge is. I adjust the invoice to reflect the charge and send off the invoice.

When the buyer pays you will receive an e-mail. Then it is time to ship.

<u>Do not ship the item until payment is received!</u>

Make sure that your package is packed well. Even if the item is not fragile it still needs to be protected. I imagine the package being tossed and thrown around as it makes its way to the destination. I imagine it possibly being exposed to rain or snow. I pack accordingly.

This means the item is wrapped in a plastic bag just in case the box leaks. If the box gets crushed I surround the item with packing material to protect it. When I shake the box the item does not rattle around. It might seem extreme but you want to do your best to ensure that it arrives in one piece. Packing and shipping are part of the selling process.

Once it is ready to go you need to print out the postage. If you are printing your postage from home you can do this through eBay. If you are sending the item via Priority Mail you can even request a pick-up from the post office.

If you are going to the post office you will need to label the package yourself. You can print out an invoice which will have the buyer's address on it. Use that to label the package.

If you do not print the postage from home you will need to manually add the shipping information to the order. I always ship using a method that has tracking. It is simple enough to add the tracking information so that the buyer (and eBay) knows the package was shipped.

Shipping from home is so much more convenient. The tracking information is automatically recorded for the buyer. I can schedule a pick-up so I do not even need to leave my house. It is easier than going to the post office and standing in line and it also costs less to do it from home. eBay sellers get a discount on the postage costs.

The final things you need to do once your package has been sent is to follow up by leaving feedback about the sale. Another smart thing to do is to take care of paying your seller fees. Go to your seller account and from there you can find out what the charge is for the sale. eBay fees are due monthly but you can pay them before the due date.

What if my item isn't selling?

If your item doesn't seem to be selling, eBay will be sending you helpful tips on how to sell it.

It is worthwhile to review their suggestions but as I have stated before, reducing your price isn't always necessary. It might not have found the right buyer.

If it has been 2 weeks without any bids or offers, it is time to re-evaluate the listing and check to see what you can change.

Maybe there is more information you can add to the listing. You might need to either add photos or take better ones. If you had listed auction style maybe trying a fixed price with best offer will sell the item.

Sometimes it is as simple as the right buyer hasn't found it.

Update your pictures. Add more descriptive words to the listing and maybe change the item title to attract buyers. Research again and this time look for how many similar items are currently listed for sale and how much money are others asking.

A few times I have undercut my selling price to make my item more attractive to a buyer. Even listing the item for $5 less than another seller will make the difference in who the buyer buys from.

I rarely offer free shipping unless I can subtract the cost of shipping from the profit from the item and still come out ahead.

I want to make money from what I sell but I am not going to lose money by offering free shipping.

There will be times when you can do everything right and the item still won't sell. Don't be discouraged by this and do not reduce the price to something that will cost you money.

Set the item aside and focus on other items. Go back to that item in a month or two and chances are you will sell it then.

There is a market for just about anything. My experience selling online has seen that. If you spend any kind of time shopping around on eBay you will discover that also.

One man's trash is someone else's treasure.

Summing it all up

I hope that this guide helps you to get started selling online. I started my "career" on the Internet by writing web content. In the beginning I mainly did "How to" articles and then I moved into selling items online to supplement my income. I have established myself as a top rated seller on eBay which is a goal that took a lot of hard work and many mistakes.

Selling online is a good way to earn some extra cash but it is not always easy money. Nothing worth anything is easy. It takes patience, organization and paying attention to what often feels like a lot of tedious details to do well selling online. It is worth it though.

Writing this book was a labor of love. I do love selling online. I enjoy the communications I have had over the years with my buyers. I love it when I get positive feedback which is a reflection of my hard work. It makes me happy when a buyer is thrilled with the item that I sell them. Often the item has sentimental value to me so it is even more comforting to know that it has found a home where it will be appreciated instead of being in a box in the attic.

The money I have earned has helped my family through some rough times and it continues to be a good source of supplemental income.

I hope that you find all the answers you need to start selling online in my book.

Check out what I'm selling at the following links.

http://www.ebay.com/usr/pmbenfield

www.etsy.com/shop/TreasuresByMimi

About the author

Priscilla is a top-rated eBay seller and also has a shop on Etsy called "Treasures by Mimi".

Since 2007 she has written web content for many different sites covering a wide variety of topics.

"Turning Your Trash Into Treasure" is her first book.

You can contact the author at priscillabenfield@gmail.com.

www.ingramcontent.com/pod-product-compliance
Lightning Source LLC
Chambersburg PA
CBHW071123280526
45787CB00003B/1146